AF316610

Ukraine is a Woman, Empathy, and the farthest boundaries

Ukraine is a Woman, Empathy, and the farthest boundaries

William F. DeVault

©2020 Venetian Spider Press™
All rights reserved.
ISBN-13: 9798999523235

To those who believe, who persist, who love.

Thank you Mariya

Contents

A very brief introduction

While many of the poems in this volume are unique in my catalog, some are included to help provide subtext and illumination for this collection. Diogenes, which contained 400 lines and more than 100 references to internal and external events and persons in my life, when taken as a monologue to inform the reader, becomes an elaborate roster of clues and views into the twisting corridors of my life, mind, and art.

Not that this detracts from the core concept and conceit of the primary works…it is merely to make certain the traveler has adequate baggage for the road,

William F. DeVault

April 1, 2026

William F. DeVault   Ukraine is a Woman…

Overture

sunflowers and grain to a horizon where blue skies meet them.
harmony and peace, history as preface, not predicate,
the ancient and the new.
the perfect built on sands of history and mystery
as a woman, complex and beautiful,
torn down yet still in touch with her heart
as she reaches out in light and silver emulsion.
the power of the promise of the rise of future generations
caught in her hair. her eyes. her surprise denials
of the truth when it manifest in her hands.

Ukraine is a woman, all elements of time and tapestry
Invoked in her thoughts, caught in the need to guard herself
as she has seen the rasping tongue of cruelty against skin
thin with pain and loss and the gloss of subterfuge glamour,
enamorment, spent on frail and fickle hearts, seeking only
to touch, not hold, settling for hryvnia not gold and jewels.
people who do not understand and demand true riches,
true treasures for measures of bitter chaff and lost dreams.
she must learn to ask for more than the scrapings of the bowl,
earning her way in heartache and found courage.

Ukraine is a Woman

like an infinite field of sunflowers, brighter than the sun,
memory made and recollected, unexpected reflections
that glisten as you listen to the silence, the gentle violence
of history and mystery, ages past and runes cast at last
to predict the future and redefine the past,
echoes of Shevchenko off the mountains invoked.

predestiny as a mockery of the clockwork impatience
that drips blood and tear and sweat, wet with awakenings
that break the unmourned mornings that suggest the blessed
in tested testaments and the remnants of our invocations
paid as reparations for mad dictators and faithless lovers
that are only here for the hryvnia in the barters.

souls flying in the shadows lying when there is a multitude
of angels angling for the corners in the cathedrals of thought,
taught to the daughters left to weep in the aftermath of wars
fought for grain and territory, the Kiev-Chernigov, Galician,
and Volhynian edifices torn down to break wills and kill
the innocents to prove virtues of beasts over priests.

the feminine endures, as it must, the winged victory of hope
and resilience. the virulence of lies and the smell of sacrifice
does not purify, does not deny, no matter how hard we try
to rise above the arduous denials of the yesterdays, in glory
she resists and persists against every cruelty avenged, lessons
taught to the children to make mortar for the walls of cathedrals.

Woman is the purpose and the plan

Fields of golden wheat and memory stretch
to all points of the compass past the horizon.
The beauty of life and of the fond remembrance
binding us to respect and to consider life.

indifference

mortals rarely care
if the unaware are crying in streets
paved innuendos.
the roadkill of memory forgotten
in revulsion and denial.

Another apple harvest passed

My solitude, it rudely backs me
into black, stacking me like
burlap sacks full of crabapples
for a numb and humbling
market of incomprehensible
merchants, chanting prices
until their tongues are numb,
struggling to find a kind of barter
smarter than subsistence.

Absent hero

you were, in so many ways, an icon.
larger than life, your words and love
shaped my youth and self-awareness.
I measured so many of my accomplishments
against your approval and love, blessings
for a sometimes fragile ego growing
in a world that can be indifferent and cruel.
in my heart, a candle burns every day
to commemorate your absence in all
but tender memories that light the darkness.

dehumanization

by race. place of birth or gender
or the transition between.
neighborhood or nation.
we are stripped of value
our true identity discounted
as the slurs spit and shrapnel
shreds our bodies.
the dead mock the dead
talk the lies shrouding
us from consequence
except for the bloodstains
transfigured to ink.
social and political expediency.

beauty is a fragrant, vagrant trap

defined by grace or face or trace of higher virtues
what draws us near is often a complex alchemy
unknown even to ourselves, attar of flowers
that in nature never survived one another
in the garden or the infinite fields of prairies
marries to their slowly shifting climate
forming their own traps of similarity
or complement to please the eye. ear. lips.
the hips do not, of their own accord, deceive
but lend themselves to self-deception,
reception assumed but never promised.

warm breeze across the fields of sunflowers

the rustle of the yellow petals and leaves.
anonymity in the infinite. freedom from complexity
the pain of isolation when the soft scent of life floats
from a Shevchenko reverie, timeless and earnest.
I have seen you in the evening, the wind in your hair
as you dance soft chaos in the face of inevitability
the sun lower in in west, the stirring of frail hairs
on your arms in the wind, granting you the grace
of childhood and the sound of the blossoms
laughing with you, echoing your joy and peace.

empathy

more than a sly sympathy, the epiphany lost on soulless intellects,
wasted and tasted in cheap communion wafers placed on your tongue
as dung on a cow path, laughter in the face of death, breath held and quelled
by the revelation of our own complicity in the crimes of which
no one is blameless. it is selfish and sorrowful to not recognize
the cognizant bindings that tie us across entangled existences
to the edge of the withered sedge, as our own fears project and protect
fragile egos against our own guilt, more than blood spilt
on Egyptian cotton sheets, quantum moments invoked
and provoked in broken kintsugi at 233 months gestation.
dare you break the seal and wake the beast
locked away for decades by will alone
atoning for the hunger that fed and misled
to the precipice of madness more than once
the entombed? inhumed with prejudice
in search of peace, bliss, and true visions
of passion oriented towards the seven powers
flowering by the stone that sealed the crypt
I hold the map and only with regret will unlock
the path of the hot gold and the bright flowers
that bow in the winds of time and remembrance.

I have left behind more than remains as the clock bends
ink-stained fingertips that slip to grip the wrists that held
the conqueror wyrm prophesied and ever-present
in the gardens of hope, coping with my own infirmities
and the cacophonous sabotage of the choir of voices
presenting choices that demand, command sacrifice
for the elevation of the sunken city of self-pity
where the lost totems live their lives for better or worse
away from the curse of madness the poet represents,
poisonous pretension and pretending an elevation
of the human condition as the thigh bones split to shards
and splinters that sustain us in winters of malcontent,
spent worshiping false idols of our own concoction
in brandywine barrels buried under the palace
we promised to our consorts and heirs, without asking
if this what they wanted. haunted by the martyrdom
left to us as inheritance for the dance of decades
we perceive in various tempo, imagination filling us
with the wine of Megiddo and the fresh fruit of Eden.
a banquet of street urchins, homeless in Southern California
but the weather is amenable and amiable, and the wind is sweet.

bury me as burned dust, crushed beneath the heel of my killer.
time demands a sacrifice, the price of living among mortals.

between

between my words you kissed me,
drowning me in electric
invocations of memory and new thoughts
twitching in anticipation.
I would suffocate, gladly,
between your elegant thighs,
binding me to a promise I never dared
to say aloud, but you heard it,
and commanded me to deliver,
if not stand, for the mattress calls
in a gentle heat.
between virtue and virulence
seen in your succubus smile
as you claim your spoils
in the soils of a garden planted
as I lay between yesterday and tomorrow
between beauty remembered and sorrows
forgotten.

empathic

even if you tell me what you are willing to reveal
I cannot know how you are feeling and what
you are enduring in your life
in the moment
in the bleak blackness behind corners
that make up your mood
rude ribbons of sharp words
anger not empathy
madness to sadness
the release of jealousy and greed

the farthest boundaries

when we were children, the edges of the universe were only
as far as we could see and comprehend.
no limits perceived, and we believed we saw the very boundaries of life
of love of truth of what was and is and would be
until we crawled out our nurseries
and the floor stretched far and away.
doors were the Pillars of Heracles.

we sought the farthest boundaries with a brave laugh.
courage was our nature. courage and curiosity.
wordless memories that stacked atop one another
like mother and brother and the smothering dark
that our fathers held at bay with strong arms
and reassuring words.
rocking chair madonnas were our faith.

before philosophy or religion, we found solace
in our simple explorations of however many senses
and pretenses we instinctively gathered
over the moments and hours and years
to build ourselves as titans amid the wastelands
we left behind, finding a blind kindness
in the mercy of our limitations.

sounds were mysteries and invitations
to explore yet further, evidence of life
and discoveries in time and in space
to be allowed for in our deepest simplicities
of our theories of everything and what is next
in every morning until mourning cloaks avenues
now buried in all but memories.

the will of a woman

Bring to the altars the offerings red
memories made in vespers unsaid
in time we've remaining, communion is bled
to be taken in tastes and remembrance.

Whispers remain in the surrogate guile
that clouds horizons anticipated, while
we bind our confessions behind sinister smile
as we walk in a crucifer's dance.

Sly sylvan moments

I have experienced that dream
the rending of veils and propriety.
That was you. Held in pretension
suspension of all excuse that might produce
a memory never born, an unworn
robe to be shed to play bed
on the rough earth beneath our feet.

Solferino Amomancies

the mythos makes it easier to retell the stories,
like proper poetry, the meter and rhyme, the glories
indicative of a preconscious sublimation of skill,
consistencies of totem and allegory, we fill
meanders with the elegance of craft, the light
of refracted truths, the vision that rends the night
even when flourished in the fantastic and romantic
for the transfigured elevation in written tantric.

Sunflowers

yellow petals and the basest of metals, a universe in borders only violated
by those who do not understand the lessons of history and the mystery
of the ferocity of pride that transcends the evil of cons and conquerors.
beauty and a bestial will to survive and thrive against the fiercest pain
visited by the vigilante violence of foreign oppressors lying to themselves
that Slava Ukraini is merely a slogan and not the stone and steel of reality.

where even women are the fiercest resistors and sisters of Athena and Mars,
clever and unrelenting on the battlefields, determined to make their mettle
match their beauty and sense of duty to their millennium of existence
no matter how bent by the brutality of foreign despots seeking to touch
the petals of heaven without understanding the ferocity of will and faith
burnt into their souls, persistance and resistance denying foreign dreams.

(r)evolution

You are a revelation. Preternatural. Even more so as you don't realize
the power you possess, I confess. Besting others effortlessly while the world
seems intent on beating you down, breaking your spirit and fracturing your soul
in so many unsubtle and unsuitable ways, karma pays and plays a cruel game.
…

find what you love and make it immortal

weeping pink and vanta black
chant, incant.
be it verb or noun
proper or improper
offered up to the Gods of religion or politic
courtly love or primordial lust
the justice of trust held high and esteemed
on purpose in purpose to propose
a new name for the rose
risen to reawaken the long taken drought
of outlandish fortunes in a land of nothingness
I remember it all
I remember you all
I remember all you dared to share
perhaps imperfectly as memory
is a mirror subject to idle sabotage
but my words are my tintypes collected
collocated
and stored for the sweet and bitter histories
mysteries of a religion of tenderness
where confessions need no penance

Dneiper

flowing like a lover's soul, born in ancient times
to bind and separate, the gate and the waterway
to foreign lands and memories. winding through
your consciousness a precious tributary to carry
you away at night to distant fantasies and rest.
testing your vesting to the fields and cities,
pities ungiven when driven wild with rains
that feed the currents against the will of those
who thought themselves the masters of nature.

an holy sin

an holy sin, the completion of the circle
consummation. conflagration. remembrance
of things yet to come.
the metal of the cage melts and Hephaestus
smelts tools and travesties
for the long trip ahead, shedding
preconceptions and memories
like waterglass against the grain,
Damascus steel and the forge or forgeries.

Peripheral vision

I dreamt of you
in colours like the moon
pale blue and cryptic whites
to curve into me in nights feral
and unforgiving

we did not know
or did we care
from where desires born
turn from our fantasies
remembrances to feed

words in ancient tongues
tongues that whisper
ancient our flesh, meshing
as we share our fires
well into the earnest night

this very night

I dreamt of you this evening
you were not here to fulfill
prophecies wishes
bright and dark
my desires lay upon you
this very night stretching time
romance affection
more than a little lust
in memorable expressions
until I woke alone

American anthemathema

The night falls
the creatures of darkness emerge
driven by hungers ignorance
fear hate, the reversion
to the revulsive impulses, betraying
values and virtues, even God,
in egocentric eccentricities.
the nobility of empathy forgotten
as darkness falls
around them
within them
history calls out another martyr
the hungry vampyrs in a dying empire
pedophilic carnivores trading their
eternal souls for the moment

monochromatic rainbows

their one-dimensional minds and hearts
dream of monochromatic rainbows
where the Sistine Chapel
had a fresh coat of eggshell landlord paint
in a world of plainsong
uninspired free verse
a universe of mediocrity

2:45 am spontaneous poem

my phase 1 alarm just went off.
the joke is on it
as I have been up for 2 hours
working out (believe it or not)
because I went to bed too early
last night.
then lay awake in a haze
of tangled synapses
trying to remember the name
for Tourette's Syndrome
and refusing to look it up
as I train my brain to obey me.
finally finding a route through
Tardive Dyskinesia
(I can explain this more fully
but I suspect you have already glazed over
on my invocation of synaptic memory theory).
I think I shall grab an early breakfast
then take a nap.

Seven Feathered Messengers of the Apocalypse

Intro:

Faerie wings beating down the wind of my exhalations
as the tiny creature, born of dreams and will, takes flight
against the indifferent sky in the darkness, surrendered
by the sun and stars, to a distant vain echo of existence.
Bursting from epic tragedy and the sparking of threads
woven into the frail fabric that can catch the reds and golds
to make the puffed downdrafts press ruby-blue feathers
into the airs, every rhythm a pulse of poetic revelation
as I match my word to the rhythms beaten to stay aloft.

Psyche

sleek and sensuous, deceptive in its earnest flutter,
a raptor and the captor of mind and belief, lost faith
and the wraith of mythic beasts made manifest in words
cured like a deep wound cleansed with a song.

Eden

watchful for the omened nest, birth and death and breath
breathed out in a trill that penetrates sorrows borrowed
by pain and gain of mysteries guarded by the field of view
focused to movement of light and flight from danger.

Panther

dark as the night, deception is her friend, fear drives her
to make her nest of lost horizons, breathing deeply
to fill her lungs and spread her slender wings to rise and fall
in an unsubtle trill with a flick of her tail to slip away in shadows.

Crimson

brash and brilliant. ruby and ripe and daring to seek what is out of reach
as she teaches her song in long sweeps of her elegant wings to glide
higher and higher, the immolation of Uriah, memories of liberty
ripped from her delicate tongue in songs of the moment and memories.

Golden

the sun rises in lemon shades and serenades both sweet and acidic,
seven powers invoked in provoked scenes of a garden where Venetian skies
size up the long odds of avian gods still drifting across the skies to smile
while they remember the angelic down we lay upon once upon a time.

Sooth

the melody of the phoenix, calling in seven art harmonies, strange runes
carved into the tree where we rested between self-deceptions, captured
and enraptured by your lazy spirals that promised nothing but regret,
wet with tears and the traces falling away as freedom is your legacy.

Firebird

plumage marking trails across the infinite sky, the fates as gates to dart through,
the art of celestial arts magnified in the lenses of your perfect eyes, mesmeric traps
for time lapse synapses firing in self-immolation to magnify your beauty
into immortality, reborn in image and word and the absurdity of resistance.

the American sepulcher

the spelling has changed:
the mourning in America
now rises as a wail for justice
denied for now
but inevitable
the rising sun of hope
equality
no matter how much dirt
is shoveled over us
our earnest prayers
lead us to redemption

Nothing begins at the beginning

The tears we'd sweated wetted and whetted
the candelabra crystal floors, making friction
a fiction as we slide down the rainbow, slow
at first, then gradually picking up speed
as we make our descent spiral a pretty dance
like a music box I gave someone a thousand
triumphant tragedies ago. Bitter thoughts
shot like artillery of a kiss paid for in patience.

Cannon fodder daughter

Remains of the deoxyribonucleic acid
lingering in every cell and memory
born to live, damned to die, a soldier
shouldering his faith and responsibilities
out of duty and love for country and family.
Whether in Afghanistan or Ukraine
the warrior's ethos leads him on and feeds
his sense of belonging on the battlefields
when all he ever really wanted was a hug
from a loving daughter and an afternoon's peace.

Slava Ukraini

Glory to the land of your birth.
Rich and historic are the forces
that release what would, in time,
a force of beauty and creativity
to conquer a poet's mind and soul
controlling the trickle of fickle blood
to surge to flood so many lives
in the revelation to affect, passion,
fashioning powerful and delicate art
of word and images, resonant remnants
we one day leave behind for futures
to find and acknowledge the elegance
of a dance in infinite fields of memory.

Where shall I begin to spin my dreams
when they are already denied, shall I be
a fickle supplicant who, spurned and turned
away from the Great Gates of Kyiv,
decides it was an illusion of virtue
unworthy of the unleashed eloquence
of dancing words that are heard in practiced
cynicism and hard won lessons of lies
designed to open your thighs but not your heart,
plagued the hideous trolls of past perditions
woven to earn and spurn the least treasures
like hryvnia coined in fool's gold and rice paper
that melts with sweat and tears and time.

Glory to you and your armored armory of
amotations and doubts abounding from the shell
of hell and fractured fields where sunflowers
grew to the horizon, where the fighters know
there is no surrender to a pretender of peace
released in ceaseless warfare to forge an
empire of pig iron and irony where heroes
stand and fall and call out to the saints
for one more day to resist with the lies
that fill ears and eyes and hearts persisting
in the belief in what was good and pure and true
still has value in the swarms of drones and bullets
sprayed like spittle from a mad dog dying.

Notwithstanding

It is not warm at the center of the storm
notwithstanding the wind blowing
there is little motion, just emotion
frozen in anticipation, hesitation
being the watchword of sentinels
charged with guarding sanity and vanity
held sacred in the defilement of hope
of promise made and unmade, fading
like a memory not so important now
that we have surrendered to despair
in the lair of lost opportunities.

Judgement

The lover trudges to the precipice at the edge of redemption
seeking to prove steadfast their heart
seeking to prove that the start
is not from the highest point
where it is all downhill from.
Broken like brittle bric-a-brac
left to be shattered beneath heels
of the endless armies of self-justifications
that in the end are just the lies we tell ourselves
when all that remains are the stains
of sloppy kisses, near misses of lips
and hips and slips of the tongue.

Simple words heard in silence

The silence of seduction, the deduction
of the suction of hungry hearts and starts
that are so far in the past that we do not remember
what we meant when we sent the flowers
and you lied they meant something other
than what the card meant and we repent
but do not know the rituals you require
before I am left to the pain and the fire

the wine at the wedding feast

was it two or three cups before Jesus showed up and fortified courage
bringing your lips to mine if but for a brush
not knowing I have rules about such things
not taking advantage of the one opportunity
I perhaps will ever be afforded to cash in
for all the emotional investments made

prime numbers against the two steps

having had my experience with dancing faeries
in the shadows of the fens when at my most
vulnerable
open to opportunity but bent back against
my own mythologies
that ultimately damn me to a different section
of the library and bookstore
with a score or more of ones and zeroes
the digital digitalis of my heart, eventually
cracking in the cold I have allowed to capture me
to rapture me
in my own eschatological pretenses
I thought I had imprisoned one side of me
but instead made the bed in brambles and shambles
of a heart forever broken, like am honorable man,
cannon fodder on a battlefield, bereft of light
captive to the dreams, the screams of the damned.

evidence of God

I find evidence of God
in the way you smile.
proof positive, that there is
something undefiled
despite the way the world spins,
often trashing hopes.
for you have that essence, prime,
surmounting slopes
that lead to the mountaintop
where there is vision
that sees beyond the moment
and finds in us one
more chance to dance with bare feet
on the soft Spring grass
and laugh like children
as the angels pass.

Faded Marble Tiles

The floor of the ballroom
where we were supposed to dance
for the gathered family and friends
has long since faded and chipped
slipped from our memories of alternate realities
where we held the course
and each other
to smother the contrary fates
that would confound us if permitted.

inexplicable

beyond the obvious attraction to your beauty
I have no rational explanation
for my dogged commitment in the face
of indifference
I have spent more than a few hours
trying to decipher the code of my coda
as I spend years as sad supplicant
at your altar
never even given a sip of wine or wisdom
enough to find the trail to the edge of reason
seasoned by so many lost causes
in my past, casting an everlasting net
into the midnight constellations
to slip amongst the stars and scars
in the carving of your graven images
to celebrate a religion of romantic
pedantic self-referencing a long forgotten
memory of love in feathers and petals.

Into the shadows and the fog

illusions resist the persistence of poetry
the popular pretense of perpetual emotions
self-referenced into affinity and infinity
the thickening of a quickening turned legend
from the simplest of chemical reactions
retractions that contradict assertions
twisted in double helix around the core
we swore allegiance and expedience to
in our bravest and most naive moments
where all we were involved retracting
reactions to unsatisfied satiety and sanity.

Acolyte in midnight silence

Nothing makes me sadder
than knowing I am not
what you want
and what you need
in your life right now.
That I will never tastes your kisses
or feel you surrender
in conquest of me as lover.
But I love,
imperfect and persistent, nonetheless.
For that is what my affection,
my passion,
and my awe
command of me.

the tale of the kitsune

bartering pieces yet unpatched in the thatched grey roof
signifying immortality
not of the sort sought by those caught in the webwork
of words, absurd and subtle, but on a plane of thought
where twelve generations of children puzzle over
hearts and parts depicted, conflicted by the seven powers
caught in a tincture bottled to draw the earnest reynard's eloquence
painting pretty word pictures in whispers
from beyond the shut door and shuttered window
the widow wept for a different partner's soliloquy

the image blurs and there are various sightings
of the number of tails this kitsune bears
as badges of longevity and magic
tragic and ridiculous. matador and bull.
the end of this world is the start of others
and the mysteries are transfigurable.
meet me on the forest, in the way the allegorist
ensures immortality for mortals
for a dram of inspired perspiration
made nutrition and contrition

the crucifer and the crucified, denied by the ignorant,
a gospel of the gods' spell propelling us to the brink
of madness born of sadness and solitude.
the isolation of the feral and the betrayed
that played out in the dance of the decades
the chance for truth portrayed in metaphors
the benediction of the vixen
the virgin and the lost spirit
twisted but unbroken
the token for the ride of the bride that never was

Diogenes

pg. 29

A light at night will cast a shade
of those who lurk in darkest grade,
against the walls, a tableau played
by actors frail and unafraid.

Weary feet now beat the stone
as penance we cannot atone,
a thinning sin reduced to dust
beneath the tread of those who trust.

Words that wrap and weave and stick
like sores upon a patient, sick,
the course and fate of this disease
is woven in our destinies.

A prophecy, a thought elusive
ought to stop the dreams, abusive.
The trojan hearse, on wheels of stone,
marks sure the road to hills of bone.

The saddest truth is yet revealed,
when earth is struck and bells are pealed.
We are but waiting for worms and kin
to strip this flesh, but leave this sin.

In whitest fog the dark remains,
a carnival for crimson stains,
and through it all we seek our path
to face our god or mortal wrath.

Beyond this dream, the shadow lurks, t
he masque of death, with purpose, smirks,
to give to us our final kiss
a bon voyage, to pain or bliss.

A tragedy in endless acts,
a comedy that warps the facts,
 story told in pantomimes
to mock the living for their crimes.

So come with me and let us seek
a chain for victors, bread for the weak,
a gift once given, now withdrawn,
and just before the waited dawn.

You ask my name, I give it free,
Diogenes, now come with me.
Just follow hard upon my tread
and we shall find an honest bed.

I weep alone within my shell
for having heard the thunder's knell
for crimson womb I could not fill
but slipped away and mocked my will.

For shadows played in theater small
to represent the part, and all,
memories made and memories
fell'd by aching arms where once they held.

The line is drawn and pulled to break
like kisses we cannot forsake,
we serve our sentences alone
for all the sins we would atone.

Where shadows fall and shades now stalk
we stand in silence, make small talk,
of smaller thoughts and smaller prayers
that shrink before the unspoke dares.

Riddles ridden to the edge of the sky
where lovers chance and lovers die
in legends and in truth to tell
when breaking neath the mystics' spell.

Failed amomancies reveal the veil,
 reveal the seal on folded sail,
that catches not the winds that brush
across the flesh of lover's flush.

Within the spell the shades will melt
to leave a skin of memories felt
and long forgotten, in perfect frame,
to be revealed in totem'd name.

Forget me not, forget me now,
a wink, I think, neath plucky brow
that raised the bar and raised the hell
and fractured me from out the shell.

Fleeing free we run to shore
to pose as Poes, and nevermore
in windows framed in curtains red
let morning sun illume a bed.

You ask my name, I give it now,
Diogenes, come with me now.
Just listen to my fading stride
that you may tell this tale with pride.

You would not lay on petals strewn
to validate my pensive ruin
and thus the tale was left to fray
a tapestry with feet of clay.

You send your scouts to mark the trail
we mark in stark with banshee's wail,
that woke the sleepers late at night
to fight a laugh at love's delight.

The pale, sweet girl with graveyard eyes
placed violets between her thighs
and called to me, to my surprise,
to take her turn at memory's lies.

And I could not resist the call,
trapped as I was, in misery's fall,
so penance did I pay for years
of anger's lash for coward's tears.

The spider sweeps with tender kiss
that bears the poison wrapped in bliss,
and draws the leper's blood to mark
a patch of moss in shaded park.

The search remains a constant quest
for hearts unplayed in passions' test
a requisite for legends bent
upon an anvil of unrest.

Brave Bragi boasts in rainbow terms
he dances well to quell the wyrms
and yet his sweat reveals his heart
is troubled by the humble dart.

Where Cupid plays as Loki's pet
to stop the heart of timeless set
and draw the wrath of bards and gods
who'd wagered on immortal odds.

That half a man can be astride
a horse, a course, a friend and bride,
remarking off the mark a curse
that spins the winds to terse reverse.

You ask my name, I shall respond,
Diogenes, back from beyond.
Take up your load and walk a ways
to take the silence from my days.

Chant the cant and chase the sky
to where a Daedalus can die
when Icarus becomes undone
by ancient evil's blotted sun.

And where and when shall stains remain
and conversely, run off in rain,
the reign of fools and regents kept
as cards to play on pauper's bet.

Tigers and the cheetahs run
for being left out of the sun,
mythology amiss, amuck,
where currencies of love are struck.

The angels weep and shed their wings
to seek in pillows golden rings
that never come until they lie
and now their histories deny.

A pampered pawn emits a yawn
and plays the matador as faun,
a piper dances panicked tune
and ponders if the end comes soon.

Brass bars that bend when muscles flex
no longer bind the blind to vex
the souls once lost at cost to cast
a final die to wager Bast.

When falls the chips to slip away
returned to fight another day
we seek the sleek in leggy taunt
that coils tight to ever haunt.

And you remain a sheltered brand
that turns to burn the holding hand
unveiled to fail upon your call
in darkened end to cloistered hall.

Remain and soothe the silent pain
in cryptic tales that mock the vain,
while I lay stones to edge the trail
in alabaster, smooth and pale.

You ask my name, and give your word –
Diogenes, your secrets heard.
Learn well the lessons that you find
along the round that much shall wind.

The lamp is lit to find the way
and to illume as if by day
the languid lurkers who repose
in tangled thorns of totem'd rose.

Sandalwood and jasmine blooms
to fill the corner of far rooms
in memory of what passed between
two lovers in the dark, unseen.

The mysteries and histories
designed to both now curse and please
the paramours and fading frauds
that sought to stride amongst the gods.

Lamps that light and lamps so bright
they blind us to the pith of night
and chase our fears back to the womb
where once we cradled naught but doom.

No cynic I, but truth does burn
its mark in stark to bid us turn
from paths of hope and prayers of love
to seek for us a prisoned glove.

The Amomancer sets the song
and we can all but sing along
until the tune unwinds the tale
of those who rise and those who fail.

Kisses cut into the thread
that winds the spindle in my head
to weave for touch and taste and scent
an image fair to represent.

Where cornered mystics miss their mark
for currencies of the coward's dark
where hides our guilt and shame and grief
and begs to buy a card's relief.

A butterfly can land for brief
and flutter by to no relief
to he who wants to see in clear
the patterns of the wings, drawn near.

You ask my name, it matters not,
Diogenes, so long you've sought.
And so the answers yet shall shade
til time will end this masquerade.

A kiss, amiss, to Delphi goes
to beg the priest to bless the rose
we left upon the bloodied sheet
from which there was no real retreat.

Cured and spurred, from pain inured,
the kitten cries, the cat has purred
and ancient tone of pleasure made
in darkened room or noon's parade.

Betrayal seems a twisted theme
a pattern not, but still a dream
too often damned by my own hand
in folly fled from final stand.

Clock work markings mock the time,
histories exposing hypocrite's crime.
Identity, a riddle wrought and writ,
read from cards of tapestry knit.

Is the price too high in wish to die
to break the bonds of ancient lie?
Must love subsist on the blood of a wrist
unpierc'd by the crucifist?

Teach to me Aphrodite's tongue
that I may speak in songs unsung,
stung like the spider, my flesh to feed
to the children of the victor's need.

The whipping boy a pose to seize
to rectify your father's disease,
penance for another's sin,
until bones crack, blacked from within.

Bury me while I still do breathe
and lay not on me plastic wreath
let history judge my laurels and crowns
as marks of the victor or the tears of clowns.

Scattered sands and withered hands
and the legacy of demanding glands,
arguing their case for war
under wedding veil in the bed of a whore.

You ask my name, I will reveal,
Diogenes, your fate to seal.
A seeker of an honest soul,
amongst the ruins I patrol.

From Jeremiah to Job and back
in the random rage of a plan of attack
that scatters not the scattershot
that marks the memory we'd forgot.

Cowards send our sons to die
and curse when we dare ask them why
they do not offer up their kin
to prove this move is not pride's sin.

Silence keeps its own respect,
to follow truths it won't inspect,
death dries the fountain where we drank
when blitzkrieg raged and bodies stank.

All I seek is a golden heart
to end this race I did not start
but which fell into unwilling lap
to link the hemispheric gap.

Weary now - my feet, they fail,
the shadow'd dawn is long to pale
and alleyway and stony street
cringe beneath my aching feet.

Diogenes, a curse and a calling,
with raped and rapid hearts now falling
like idols I never erected, suspected
by the ignorant, but undetected.

Summon the priest and give him the word,
spoken in silence, it lingers unheard,
absurd and mocking, stalking the frames
of our doors and our windows, exposing our shames.

I would find new nemicorn, illusion to dispel,
but would I leave menagerie behind, in hell,
rejecting the mantle of Orpheus, to refuse
to follow to the inevitable the Hero's bruise?

I cannot end this futile walk
that makes heads shake and gossips talk
while there is hope or dream or prayer
of finishing this destined dare.

You ask my name, so listen well,
Diogenes, your fate shall tell.
To take my quest and carry on
when bones are all the greet the dawn.

What of the child who has yet to learn
of that which bring their heart to burn?
What of the lovers, lost in the fire
that sparked in dark with wild desire?

Where shall I fall and to what cause
will I surrender, will I give pause,
when all around the pyres burn
to invocate for my return?

We must endure, we must ensure
that purpose to our path is pure,
and yet we cannot know the string
that pulls our hearts through everything.

Surreal, I feel, and yet I touch
the earth and sky with hands and such
I follow the precognizant memory
that was born before the Midgaard tree.

Split in twain and yet again, cut,
the angels caught in savage rut
cannot redeem beyond their fight
when the victims judge the wrong and right.

Carry back the fallen. carry them back,
to where the colours course from within black,
and turn to white in spectrums new
that harbour stones in the ruby blue.

Forgive me for my final sins,
last moments of rebellion, it begins
and ends in ignorance and arrogance,
this fated, sated, inflated dance.

The trance state transcends and God befriends
those whose action no one defends,
for in the end we are all corruption,
from conception through deception to absorption.

Drag dragons from their lair and care
to make their stare an icon to your dare to tear
scales for the epaulets of Orion,
child of the fates, the unheralded scion.

You ask my name, have you not heard,
Diogenes, this is my word.
Do not take issue with the goal,
unless you would deny your soul.

Prepare the path and take a rest
you'll find one mind is not a test
but seek the inner populi
your vox to vex your memory.

And I recall the every touch
of those who meant so very much
when words were tokens for the kiss
that yet unclaimed returns to this.

All the widows, all the saints,
all that holy water taints,
blood and flesh and sweat and tears
that paint a portrait of the years.

The lamp grows heavy with the time
and I have not yet ended the climb
up to the tower where I may see
the deserts and the Western sea.

Where tears remain to salt the flood
that could not seal the seeping blood
of sacrifices made for words
to cats and bats and stones and birds.

Lips and hips and fingertips
exploring my hearts each eclipse
when God remains to curse and frown
each flower plucked and then cast down.

Nunc dimittis? I won't depart
without some answers for my heart
of who was false and who was true
and if I learned from what I knew.

Dreamers dance like angels die,
pinheads that dread the soft reply
of feet and wings and subtle touch
that topple temples so, so much.

Leathery and feathery wings are spread
into the wind, upon a bed
where heroes sleep with cowards, fled,
from purpose and to mock the dead.

You ask my name, I now reply,
Diogenes, now tell me why
I cannot find and cannot claim
an honest heart in my domain.

Remember me to perfidy –
remember me to virtue, see,
and recollect all that you saw
that bent the thrust of moral law.

When couer rage fails and flesh will fade
we'll sing a final serenade,
made of words and made of coins
extracted from the virgin's loins.

And I will spend not penny one
until the next song has begun
for I am not a rich man, yet,
I give it all to pay your debt.

Immortal dragons, standing stones,
we sit in pits with ancient bones
and argue not was yet shall be
but over arcane history.

My child, I wish that you would know
all that I've seen, without the blow
of falling hard against the earth,
inheriting the hard knocked birth.

You ask me for my blessing, now,
without the wisdom to know how
to spend the power you would request
without the proof of loving's test.

Show to me your worthy heart
then take and my staff, let us depart
to separate roads in separate spheres
and vivisect our joy and tears.

Present to me your evidence
of all you are, know no suspense,
just open wide your soul to me
that I may pass with dignity.

And knowing that my line maintains
in spite of all my failing stains,
accept the truth that fail we must
and yet again we rise from dust.

You ask my name, it matters non,
Diogenes, until I'm gone
will well suffice to be my brand
while I am dwelling in this land.

Passages of Time in Words said to Me

I. Psyche

"I don't want to see the man I love
grow old and bitter
because poetry is never coming back."

Your words. Not mine.
My words were carefully chosen
in a threnody against past affections.

I have my moments, of course,
where I wish a well-crafted and resonant villanelle
could sell well enough to buy a house.

A house like the one I gave to my first wife
when I bet my heart and art on a passing fancy
(not mine, but another's) and found my way to the angels.

II. Brigit

"Come here," you said, in a red-headed growl of desire.
I wasn't about to argue, consumed by my own ardor -
even awe of this goddess of consummate fire
stretched out before me like a new frontier to explore.

III. a host of ghosts

…so many times the confession door was locked from the inside
and I was not given vital information before the rodeo.
by then, too late, as patterns of imprinting burned
with hormonocentric permanence bound me
with damn near immutability
with a stage-two illusion of romance.

IIII. Leopard

"You'd take a bullet for anyone."
That ended the argument as a simplistic statement on my ethos
tried to guilt-filter the very essence of who and what I am,
for better or worse, had made you strip naked and come on to me on the road
just outside of Tucson, with you wired on scoops of pharmaceuticals,
and you convinced me, eventually, that I was more than a deus ex machina
for fleeing home and your city of burned bridges and disappointments.

V. White Sunday

"I meant it when I said it."
of course the irony of you saying it
was not lost on me, the cost to me
was felt deeply in the velvet folds of my heart
where I had set aside pride and possibilities
to, not pursue, but follow an orphaned offer
because I did not understand that to some people
words lack permanence, like cheeseburger kisses
and fellatio for a lobster. and three black diamonds.

and the violence of indifference.

VI. Psyche II

"but I might die tonight."
I know you were just quoting Cat Stevens,
but the message was intimate and urgent.
beautiful validation for the petals to reach out
and draw the nourishment from the sun and air.
I admit, when the sky is still and I am contemplative
I recall not just your words, but your expression
and the sweet, urgent, tenderness of the day
when I had no defenses. and didn't want them.

VII. Heresy

"you don't need to be in love to love."
I believed, I was relieved, yet I grieved the fading lights
against the venomous sun, burning a thatch work patch work
to shield us from the falling stars we threw into the sky to die.
that there should be Diogenes' sister, in denim skirt and flowers
flowers flowers everywhere, not just your renegade air.
the petty, sweaty illusions that pull groin and gravity
to draw us inexplicably together.
I do believe in love at first sight, even if I fight against it,
a trapped, sapped animal, with just enough strength to pull free,
even if leaving a metaphorical leg or segment of memory.
I am a romantique. waiting in a garden that is scented
with the flowers and seven powers that have torn and reborn
a grave slave to the bloodlust and tender thrust awakening dust
in a crypt that has never held anything but the dreams of the damned
and the passions that only intensify in the abattoir of every lie I've ever been told.
I am the priest and the heretic. the lover and the hermit. the minstrel and martyr.

About the Author

William F. DeVault has, in his creative run (so far) amassed tens of thousands of poems (and those are just the ones that passed first reading). He has published over 30 books, received his unfair share of sobriquets, and performed his poetry all over the continental United States and throughout cyberspace. He has read in churches, bars, parks, schools, libraries, and brothels.

Married twice, divorced twice, but still the romantic optimist, he has fathered three children in whom he is well pleased, and mentored dozens of poets. He founded and lead the **Romantic and Erotic Poetry Group** for America Online, and that service's **Passionate Craft** poetry workshop.

He was named the **Romantic Poet of the Internet** by Yahoo in 1996 and the **US National Beat Poet Laureate** by the National Beat Poetry Foundation for 2017-2018. Some consider him the **Poet Laureate of the Internet** for his presence and pioneering use of the internet during and even before the mid-1990's. He is a founding member in the **Rolling Stock Poets**.

www.ingramcontent.com/pod-product-compliance
Lightning Source LLC
Chambersburg PA
CBHW081356150726
48196CB00005BA/516